SUGAR-FREE SWEET TALK

A collection of verse written by a person with diabetes for people with diabetes and their caregivers

Jim Meehan

All proceeds will be used to find a cure for diabetes

Copyright 2009 Jim Meehan
All rights reserved.
No part of this manuscript shall be produced or transmitted
in any form or by any means, electronic or mechanical,
including photocopying, recording or by any information or retrieval system,
without written permission from Jim Meehan.

Send all enquiries to:
Jim Meehan
One Talent Plus Way
Lincoln, Nebraska 68506
United States of America

e-mail jmeehan@talentplus.com

This book is dedicated
to Stacie Post, a beautiful
ten-year-old girl from
Lincoln, Nebraska, who
has Type I diabetes.*

Stacie was my Youth Ambassador for the
Juvenile Diabetes Research Foundation's
Ride to Cure adventure through Death Valley on
23 October, 2004.

It is also dedicated to all those coping with diabetes and for all those living with, supporting, or in other ways helping them.

*For readers who are not familiar with the terms Type I and Type II diabetes, people diagnosed with Type I diabetes need to inject insulin into their bodies in order to stay alive, as their own supplies of insulin are inadequate or lacking due to problems with the organ that produces their insulin, namely their pancreas. People diagnosed with Type II diabetes have deficiencies with either the functioning or the quality of their insulin. In certain cases people with Type II diabetes can manage their condition by diet and exercise alone or by diet and exercise plus special drugs. However, should these measures fail, then, they too, will need to inject insulin into their bodies to stay alive and will be re-designated as people with Type I diabetes.

Contents

Preface 7
Release – A Beginning 11

Part One – Love

You Can't Say It In One 15
Love In Action 15
Armless Hugs 16
Enough Is Enough 17
One Self 18
The Other Self 18
Revolve Into Love 18
Longing 19
Love's Priority 19
Through Love 19

Part Two – Trust

Total Trust 23
A Lover's Paradoxical Plea 24
Belonging 25
Obsessed 26
Charity Begins At Home 27
Show Your Hand 27
Trust Or Bust 27

Part Three – Opposites

Insight 31
Good Ideas - Dead Or Alive 31
Before After Before 32
More Is Less 34
Less Is More 34
The Breath Of Life 35
Opposites 35

Part Four – Growth

Flow 39
Reality 39
The Selfish Gene 40
An Egocentric's Epigram 41
Smile Inside 41
Descartes Extended 42
Autumn's Renewal 43
Three's A Crowd 44
Teenagers Are Tops 44

Part Five – A Search For Meaning

Pray Hear. 47
Being In Being 48
Divine Designs?. 49
A Citizen Of Utopia. 50
Roses In December 51
Significance. 51

Part Six – Empathy

Empathetic Steps 55
Empathy Or Sympathy? 55
Hearts Have Reasons. 56
Reasons Have Hearts Too 57
Heartfelt Empathy 58
A Question Of Thanks 59
About Relating. 60
Empathy. 61
There's More 62

Part Seven – Action

Walk The Sweet Talk 65

Release – An Ending 67

Acknowledgments 69

Preface

On 24 March, 1996, the telephone rang just as my wife, Maureen and I were about to leave for a dinner to celebrate her birthday. A concerned doctor informed us that my sugar levels were dangerously high and that blood tests confirmed my initial suspicions, that I was a person with Type II diabetes. Over the next few months, my world was turned upside down as I learned how to cope with this chronic auto-immune disease. Since then, a strict regimen of diet and exercise has helped me to control the adverse effects of the disease.

Conservative estimates indicate that at least 194 million people world-wide are affected by this chronic condition, and this figure is rising dramatically. More priority needs to be given to finding a cure for this debilitating illness.

Since moving to the United States, I have, in some limited way, become involved with the work of the Juvenile Diabetes Research Foundation International (JDRF), an association which is dedicated to finding a cure for diabetes. Such a cure will relieve the suffering of children with Type I diabetes.

While biking through Death Valley in October 2004, along with 349 other riders, who were fundraising for the JDRF, I considered whether there was any other way of helping to raise money to find a cure which would help children who need to take daily injections of insulin. I decided to pull together a collection of my verses into one volume called "Sugar Free Sweet Talk" and donate all proceeds to those associations interested in working to help people coping with diabetes.

Thank you for your support.

Jim Meehan
January 2009

Speak softly and sweetly.
If your words are soft and
sweet, they won't be hard
to swallow if you have to
eat them.
> *James Thurber*

Do all you can,
With what you have,
In the time you have,
In the place you are.

> *Nkosi Johnson*

Release – A Beginning

There's something inside me that wants to get out,
Like oil under pressure, steam wanting a spout.
It's stirring inside and it's looking for words,
It's got something to say and it wants to be heard.

After some struggle and after much fumbling,
On to the page the words come tumbling.
The result when editing and proofing cease,
"Sugar-Free Sweet Talk"…
                             … a poetic release …

PART ONE
Love

You Can't Say It In One

You can say it in two,
"Love you."

You can say it in three,
"I love thee."

You can say it in four,
"I love you more."

You can say it 'til numbers and words have gone.
But you can't say it in one.

Love In Action

Loving others brings out the best in us.
Loving is what loving does.

Armless Hugs

Seeing you there sleeping, I swell with pride.
At such times, I've learned to hug you with my arms by my side.

When away from you, traveling world-wide,
Yet again, I've learned to hug you with my arms by my side.

Often yearnings to hold you are denied,
And once more, I turn and hug you with my arms by my side.

Sometimes I realize I'm not fooling you when I hide
My real emotions and hug you with my arms by my side.

My guilt gives way to your laughter and smiles,
And I am drawn to your arms, which are always open wide.

Enough Is Enough

You have always been my enough.
I never expected you to be perfect.
People are not made of such sweet stuff.
In function or form free from any defect.

Thank you for accepting me as your enough.
For allowing me sometimes to get it wrong.
For selectively calling my bluff,
Whenever my dances did not match my songs.

One Self

Investing in others for their sake always results in a hidden return.
If you and I are in some sense one, then loving you is loving me in turn.
Loving helps us both to grow, but fear and hate diminish us.
Love in action is the way to go for flourishing finishes.

The Other Self

The effects of altruism and self-interest are the same.
In giving ourselves to others our true selves we gain.

Do we need to turn our world the right side up,
And see the love that permeates it?
Then, drink deeply from love's bottomless cup,
And live love. Is that life's secret?

Longing

When you're out of sight, but still deep in my heart.
Telecommunications only meet my needs in part.
In this partial state of languish
Craving the most intimate form of body language
Your sensuality stirs my passions, which stir my soul.
Touch and smell, too, make us whole.

Love's Priority

Most philosophies of life and religious messages
    can be reduced to a simple art.
Love self and other sentient beings with head, hands and heart.
Happiness is love's outcome and not its start.

Through Love

Beyond loving there is no greater thing we can do.
When we're through loving, then we're through!

PART TWO
Trust

Total Trust

I mean you no harm,
I seek your greatest good.
Come, take me by the palm,
We'll see the stars and not the mud.
We'll see the doughnut and not the hole,
We'll walk that extra mile,
And adopt a more positive role.
No longer half dead, but fully alive.

I mean you no harm,
I seek your greatest good.
Come, take me by the arm,
We'll understand, then be understood.
We'll find ourselves in each other,
And lose ourselves there too.
The mystery of "I" – "other,"
One entity, yet two?

I mean you no harm,
I seek your greatest good.
In cold weather, I'll keep you warm.
When hungry I'll give you food.
My life is filled with calm,
As it is fully understood,
Yes…
You mean me no harm,
You seek my greatest good.

A Lover's Paradoxical Plea

Let us lose ourselves once more in love tonight,
Explore a world of bliss and put our cares to flight.
Let us each become part of a greater whole,
Through the furious fusion of body and soul.

Let us find ourselves once more in love tonight,
Lift the blinds that mar the moments of clear insight.
Let us become more open and thus enable
Truth to replace what is false, fact what is fable.

Belonging

What we have, you and I, is something very special.
You know what I mean.
That longing when you're not here
That longing when you are near.
That longing night and day
That longing to hear what you say.
That longing to feel your touch…

…That longing…

That longing to give you so much.
That longing that you'd hear what I say.
That longing that won't go away.
That longing when you are near
That longing when you're not here.
You know what I mean.
What we have, you and I, is something very special…

Obsessed

Steeped in my work or out walking,
I often call you to mind,
And take pleasure in guessing,
Just how you're spending your time.

When lost in a world of ideas,
With my head high in the clouds,
Your face suddenly appears –
Your voice not terribly loud.

When wrapped in the warmth of your body,
With your will welded to mine,
Lovers meant always to be,
For all, yes, all of our time.

Charity Begins At Home

Before we can love others, that is,
    help them achieve their greatest good,
We need first to love ourselves and ourselves have been loved.

Show Your Hand

Babies emerge from the womb into the light,
With fists clenched, locksmith tight.
Let's hope when into their tombs they later slide,
A life of giving has stretched their hands open wide.

Trust Or Bust

What when absent makes a relationship go bust?
What if not found means a relationship is lost?
What is not only desirable, but also a must?
The cementing ingredient is mutual trust.

PART THREE

Opposites

Insight

Often when the commonplace is touched by the
 hand of a genius, great beauty appears.
Often simplicity lies at the root of humankind's greatest ideas.
Often reality is masked by layers of sophisticated intellectual veneers,
 awaiting an incisive mind to penetrate and clear.

Good Ideas - Dead Or Alive

"Avoid the dead ideas of the living and follow the living ideas of the
 dead," he said.
Better still he added …
"Follow the living ideas of the living along with the living
 ideas of the dead."

Before After Before

Before the storm, the lull.
After empty, full.
Before the fall, the decline.
After clouds, sunshine.
Before after, before.
After uncertain, sure.
Before tears, laughter.
After before, after.
Before joy, pain.
After sun, rain.
Before hope, despair.
After here, there.
Before stop, go.
After to, fro.
Before found, lost.
After free, cost.
Before an up, a down.
After a smile, a frown.
Before go, wait.
After love, hate.

Before happy, sad.
After sane, mad.
Before clean, mess.
After sin, blessed.
Before laugh, weep.
After tired, sleep.
Before war, peace.
After famine, feast.
Before drink, thirst.
After better, worst.
Before lost, keep.
After look, leap.
Before pain, joy.
After fail, try.
Before all, none.
After rain, sun.
Before tall, small.
After the rise, fall.
Before lover, friend.
After beginning, end.

More Is Less

More knowledge, more of the universe shows,
And the greater the circle of our ignorance grows.

The more we know, the more we know we
                don't know.
True humility is achieved by those who know
                this is so.
Not by those who see themselves as lower than
                low!

As an electric light in the darkness grows,
More is lit, yet we see more shadows.

Less Is More

Life is so mysterious that we are able to say
That the value of living could be seen to lie not
In the number of breaths we take, as we're taught,
But rather in the number of times our breath is taken away.

The Breath Of Life

Without a doubt...
    My body will die if I only breathe in and
        don't breathe out.

It is indeed also true...
    That I'll die as a person if I think only
        of me and little of you.

Opposites

When very happy, we often cry,
To grow, to self, we must die.
Our bodies are changing, but we are the same.
All around is the permanence of change.
Value from suffering often emanates
Like the perfume of crushed roses or wine from crushed grapes.

PART FOUR
Growth

Flow

It's never too late to relate,
You're never too old to unfold.
Just open your heart,
That'll do for a start,
Let go. Don't try to control.

Reality

A blind man and a deaf man walked through a storm,
But their meanings and feelings were not the same.
Different pictures in different frames?

One man's thunder and another's flashes are just as true.
It's by sharing our pieces that we gain a full view
From partial pictures of me, partial pictures of you.

The Selfless Gene

What do those scientists really mean,
Talking of the selfish gene?
When a gene has no mind at all,
A mere biological billiard ball,
Cued by external forces to convey
Its structured message in a pure functional way!

Genes cannot decide to replicate,
Inform, split or duplicate,
Mindlessly affecting and being affected by environmental laws,
Is not sufficient to explain their mutational flaws.
Another factor turns predictable patterns into a mess –
And that ingredient is known as randomness.

It is not a choice between born or bred, innate or acquired,
Of being permanently fixed by the way we've been genetically wired.
Our endowment influences our environment and vice versa,
Nurture affects nature and nature affects nurture.
We are not totally determined by the genes we inherit,
Influenced yes! But free choices need to be taken on their merits.

An Egocentric's Epigram

Some people don't really seem to bother
Living in the world of "I" – "other."
They really appear content to be
In the lonely world of "I" – "me."
Only ever saying "hello"
To their only companion, their own ego.

Smile Inside

Smile inside! Put a stop to that self-pitying sob!
True happiness is, above all else, an inside job.

Descartes Extended

I scheme and I plan.
I search and I scan.
I think, therefore, I am.

I laugh when I can.
I cry though a man.
I feel, therefore, I am.

I work with my hands.
My word is my bond.
I act, therefore, I am.

I think, feel and act. Therefore, I am!

Autumn's Renewal

Is it because Winter nears,
That most trees shed their leafy tears?
Is it because Summer's gone,
That it's no longer warm?
Is it because the trees are tired,
That they can't hold their blooms so long?
Or is it that they require,
More fresh sap to keep them strong?

Many birds feel the Fall
As nature's sign to take the air
And answer this instinctive call
To seek warmth and sun elsewhere.
Leaving us behind to stare
At the browns, yellows and gold.
That remind us every year
That we, like trees, grow old.

Autumn's a time to take stock of time
And retreat from life's pressures,
To renew rhythm and rhyme
And realize life's treasures.
Autumn signals Winter's cold
And nature slows down its pace.
Shorter days and longer nights unfold,
Less daylight in which to race.

Three's A Crowd

Communication is one of humankind's obsessions.
What is needed is less mass media and more
    two-way, one-to-one sessions.

Teenagers Are Tops

Teenagers are like tops spinning.
Too much parental interference can lead to a fall.
What they need is balanced steering,
To help them keep their eye on the ball.

PART FIVE

A Search For Meaning

Pray Hear

Are you really there?
Are people talking to fresh air
When addressing you in prayer?

Is anybody home?
Are people talking to themselves
Or leaving messages on an imaginary answer phone?

Seriously, seriously,
Have you been trying to get through to me
Without making a forced entry?

If you really can't appear
Then speak I'm all ears
But I've been listening for many years.

How do you relate?
I suppose I'll have to wait.
Time's passing it's getting late.

If love is who you really are,
I don't have to go very far.
I can do that for sure.

Are you really there?
Am I just talking to fresh air?
Pray, what is going on here?

Being In Being

Often instinctive drives compel us to explore the cold nonhuman universe,
And our radio telescopes unearth strange and mysterious events.
Is all this chance chaos or is the discovered order something far worse,
An explanation our intellect invents?

Are we God-created or randomly evolved from primeval slime?
Are we on earth to fulfill some proper purpose,
Or just a paleontologist's enigma, lost in eons of time,
Clumsy clowns in a cruel, cognitive circus?

In being in being philosophers of East and West can unite,
Introspection and altruism can almost become the same.
The idea of loving self and others as one being appears to be quite right,
For it gives life meaning – an ultimate aim.

Divine Designs?

Suddenly something in my brain goes click,
A pattern is perceived as if by magic.
Clouds suddenly reveal a face,
My mind monitors patterns in space.

Why do things look as they do?
Do I see objects and colors the same as you?
What is figure? What is ground?
How are parts and whole together bound?

Sometimes we notice hidden features by chance,
A sudden movement, a different glance.
Sometimes others advise where and how to view,
Leaving the resolution up to me and you.

Many philosophers who have studied Greek and Latin,
Fail to see in life's events any pattern.
People and their history are available to all,
To some providing openings, to others merely a wall.

What in the end causes us to believe?
What makes us adopt the lives we lead?
Does faith turn designs embedded in reality
Into divine designs by seeing them supernaturally?

A Citizen Of Utopia

Someone who thinks none harm,
        wills none harm,
        says none harm,
        does none harm.

Someone who in themselves feels warm,
        is warm,
        to their neighbor warm,
        to their family warm.

Someone whose inner light shines bright and takes
        delight in the sharing of their flame.
Someone who makes a difference –
        a candle lighting other candles –
Yet whose brilliance remains the same.

Such people, though few in number, are not mere
        citizens of imagination.
They mingle among us, and pre-occupied we let their
        deeds and influence escape our due
        consideration.

Roses In December

I'm glad we've evolved the ability to remember,
So that we, in the North, can have roses in December.
Just think of all the things we might recall,
When in the seasons of our lives we reach the Fall.

Now is the time to fill our memory banks,
By helping others and giving thanks
For the opportunity to do a little good,
And collect one more unforgettable rosebud.

Significance

Do we all need to feel significant?
Is it part of the human predicament?

PART SIX
Empathy

Empathetic Steps

When stepping on each other's toes, our shoes need not lose their shine.
When walking in another's shoes, I must first get out of mine.

Empathy Or Sympathy?

"Your wounds deeply wound me."
Emotional empathy mainly.

"You have my pity."
Sympathy to a high degree.

"Your situation is clear to me."
Rational empathy mostly.

"I wouldn't do that if I were you."
Neither of the two.

"I feel your pain."
Emotional empathy again.

"I see it the way you see it.
I feel it the way you feel it.
And I'll help you in any way I can."
Now that's total empathy, man!

Hearts Have Reasons

Hearts have reasons, not so easy to find.
Body and mind being so inextricably entwined.
This is not an area of clear black and white.
Deep in the psyche, feelings and thoughts merge and unite.
Gut reactions could be nut reactions in disguise.
Intuition, polysyllogisms cut down to size.
Impulse, the brain's parallel processing gone wild.
Spontaneous creativity, reason's real child.
Hearts have reasons which we can't always find.
As an engine is to power, likewise is the body to the mind?

Reasons Have Hearts Too

Reasons have hearts too.
Feelings can affect the way we think.
And also what we say and do,
Reasons, heart, and actions inter-link.

Minds have biological roots,
Yet they produce surreal images,
Pink elephants in green hobnailed boots.
In memory, real horses pull real carriages.

Is there also a soul
Generating ideas free from time and space?
An all embracing, spiritual whole,
That makes the human race race?

Heartfelt Empathy

Your pain and joy in my heart.
This is both a skill and an art.

To really feel what you're going through
And see how closely I can come to you.

I'll listen actively to what you say
And, non-judgmentally accept all you convey.

I'll do whatever you require,
Your greatest good is all I desire.

Your sorrows I yearn to take away,
And give you some sun in which to make some hay.

The more of you I understand,
The better fashioned my helping hand.

A Question Of Thanks

How often do we express our thanks and let people know that they are really appreciated?
Can we thank too much or do we leave some helpers underestimated?

Do those who have been most influential in our lives know how grateful we actually feel?
What specific actions do we take, to let them know that our gratitude is real?

Do we take all the people who make our lives worthwhile in little ways for granted?
The person opening the door, the person who makes sure our shrubs are properly planted?

What expression is best used to recognize all our gifts and the deeds that others do?
How about, a sincerely given and heartfelt,

> "Thank you"

Made more audible with acts of service too?

About Relating

To relate to others, I have no doubt,
Unless we go within, we'll go without.
Unless we know how we're feeling and what we're thinking about,
Actions' true meanings we'll never fathom out.
Was that a bribe or was it a gift?
Is that certain smile, really, a downer with a facelift?
To relate to others of this I have no doubt,
Unless we go within, we'll go without.

Empathy

If we could listen actively to our every word and sigh,
Would I see you, as you do, and you me as I?

If we could watch each other carefully, when we laugh and cry,
Would I feel, as you feel, and you sense as I?

If we could walk in each other's shoes and not be passers-by,
Would I see the world, as you do, and you the world as I?

Active listening and self-disclosure will lead by and by,
To a deeper understanding – seeing more than eye-to-eye.

There's More...

There's more to you than meets the eye,
There's more than tears when you cry.
There's more to you than what you show,
There's more to you than others know.
There's more to words than what is said,
There's more to following than being led.
There's more to kissing than touching lips,
There's more to satire than pointed quips.
There's more to alms than in the giving,
There's more to life than just in living.
There's more to action than the deeds,
There's more to words than what we read.

PART SEVEN
Action

Walk The Sweet Talk

When many people hear the word diabetes
They first think of people who can't eat "sweeties."
Some of them have the firm opinion, I'm sure,
That insulin is diabetes' certain cure.

Others who appear to have more of a clue
On this subject don't make one plus one equal two,
Describing one type of diabetes as being "mild"
Which drives medical experts "mildly" wild.

To help people take a more realistic view,
I call on sensible readers like you.
For the only way that we will ever relax –
Is when we feel that people understand the facts.

Once diagnosed, the daily battle begins,
Which no one afflicted ever fully wins.
At best they can keep the worst effects at bay
By controlling blood sugars every minute of every day.

Body cells need sugar to keep them alive,
And to give us energy and essential drive.
In healthy people the answer lies within
The pancreas and the hormone insulin.

Insulin helps sugar move into cells from the blood,
So it doesn't build up in your veins like mud.
Without adequate insulin people die.
Their bodies starve while their blood stands by.

Type I diabetes is the class we give,
To those who need injected insulin to live.
Others whose insulin is good to some degree,
Go into the broad Type II category.

Both types are similar and have one and the same goal.
To keep their blood sugars under tight control.
Injected insulin is a crutch, not a cure!
It merely keeps Type I's away from death's door.

Some Type II's use pills to boost their ailing insulin.
Others with diet and exercise can keep trim.
But whatever means all types use,
The fight for blood sugar control is one they can't lose.

Diabetes is a hard burden for children to carry,
So we adults must not dilly and dally
When it comes to funding the founding of a cure
We've got to win this particular war.

So please support a cause or help a foundation,
And bring the benefits of research to every nation.
And you'll bring many a smile to many a face.
There are 194 million of us in the human race.

Thank you.

Release – An Ending

It's over now, but will I ever convey
Its intensity and what it wanted to say?
The next time my inner pot begins to boil,
I hope my words will come through much richer soil.

As thoughts, feelings and experience increase
Life's expression becomes an ongoing …
                                       … poetic release …

Acknowledgments

Special thanks to my wife, Maureen, for her inspiration, encouragement and counsel and to my daughter Larissa, for her love and strength of character. Much gratitude is extended to the highly industrious and charmingly mischievous Rhonda Green Whitlow for typing the initial manuscript, to the ever creative Erin Jansen who provided the original cover, and to all the other associates and board members of Talent Plus Inc., a human resources consultancy based in Lincoln, Nebraska, with whom I work. Talent Plus has been a very generous sponsor for many fundraising efforts and projects aimed at helping people who are coping with diabetes. Indeed, Talent Plus has borne the costs of publishing this work and encouraged Cydney Koukol from their marketing team to bring the project to completion.

Acknowledgment is also given to all those people who have acted as proofreaders and to those whose lives have provided the stimuli which prompted me to try to capture their values in verse. From among them, I would like to single out Stacie Post whose courage in handling the complications of Type I diabetes never ceases to amaze. Without her example, this project would not have proceeded. Also, much appreciated was the valuable editorial input of Matt Mason, an accomplished Nebraska poet.

In addition, I would like to thank those in various associations and societies who are seeking a cure for diabetes or are otherwise involved in helping people with the illness. In particular, I would like to make a special mention of Deborah Gokie, the Executive Director of the Lincoln Chapter of the Juvenile Diabetes Research Foundation International (JDRF), who responded so enthusiastically to the original idea. Of great value are my memberships of Diabetes UK and the American Diabetes Association and I would encourage people to support these organizations.

Finally, on behalf of all of us coping with diabetes, I would like to thank all the readers who purchased a copy of "Sugar Free Sweet Talk." By doing so, you are helping in a tangible way to both find a cure for this chronic condition and also to bring assistance to all present and future sufferers of the disease as all proceeds will go to seeking a cure.